"To be truly modern we must come to terms with our tradition."

Octavio Paz

MEXICAN
CONTEMPORARY

HERBERT
YPMA

STEWART, TABORI & CHANG
NEW YORK

PAGES 2–3
The drama of José de Yturbe's architecture is enhanced by his use of strong color. Here, the walls of the courtyard in his own Mexico City house have been painted bright yellow.

PAGES 4–5
Stone steps are a ubiquitous feature of Mexican architecture, both ancient and contemporary. Architect José de Yturbe has combined this tradition with indigenous pottery and the native love of color to create a powerful Mexican still life.

PAGES 6–7
Yellow, pink, and blue are the colors of Mexico. Architect Ricardo Legorreta used a deep blue color to paint a pair of intersecting walls in one of the many courtyards of the Hotel Camino Real in Mexico City.

PAGE 8
Terra-cotta pots in the corner of a courtyard were first arranged in this way by Luis Barragán. Today, architect José de Yturbe continues the tradition. Enormous clay pots such as these were originally used by the

Spanish as ballast for their ships on the voyage to the New World. Laden with gold, silver, and other treasures, the vessels did not need additional ballast on the return journey, and the pots were left behind in Mexico.

PAGE 12
*A bright blue wall and an **ojo de buey** ("bull's eye") window recall the architecture of the **granarias** of early Colonial haciendas and reflect architect Manuel Mestre's childhood memories of growing up on a sugar hacienda.*

For Danielle

© 1997 Herbert Ypma

First published in Great Britain in 1997 by Thames and Hudson Ltd, London

Published in 1997 and distributed in the U.S. by
Stewart, Tabori & Chang,
a division of U.S. Media Holdings, Inc.
575 Broadway, New York, NY 10012

Distributed in Canada by General Publishing Co. Ltd.,
36 Lesmill Road, Don Mills, Ontario, Canada M3B 2T6

Library of Congress Catalog Card Number: 96-72196
ISBN: 1-55670-557-3

Printed in Singapore
10 9 8 7 6 5 4 3 2 1

CONTENTS

INTRODUCTION

13

1

ORIGINS

the hacienda

cultural revolución

casa barragán

15

2

INTERIORS

contemporary color

splendid magnitude

serene geometry

las palapas

tactile texture

minimal colonial

modern mythology

43

3

COLORS

color fiesta

113

4

INGREDIENTS

tin-glazed tiles

creative clay

127

5

VIRTUOSI

mexico moderno

141

BIBLIOGRAPHY

157

SOURCE GUIDE

158

INTRODUCTION

"The most vital country of the Americas," is how visionary architect Richard Neutra once described Mexico.

Mexico has it all. Ancient mythology, indigenous craft and indigenous color, the silence of Catholic cloisters and convents, the precise geometry of pre-Hispanic cultures, the tranquility of the transplanted Moorish courtyard, the magnificent scale of Colonial haciendas—all set against the natural beauty of a vast landscape studded with darkly brooding volcanoes.

Like pieces of an intricate mosaic, these cultural treasures comprise a sensual and exotic heritage that continues to shape the way the nation expresses itself. This majestic legacy has not been relegated to a dusty corner of some museum. Instead, all these elements "sown by time and history" continue to play a vital role in contemporary art, architecture, and design. The result is a captivating juggling act between innovation and tradition that Nobel-Prize-winning author Octavio Paz once described as "an example of how to employ our popular tradition with intelligence."

In a sense what Paz refers to is a layering process. Artists and artisans of each successive generation add their own tier of influences and ideas. In Mexican architecture, the defining features remain, as ever, the courtyard, the wall, and the use of color. But to these ingredients architects and designers are bringing further innovations in scale and texture, creating spaces of massive volume, punctuated by extraordinary surfaces of rusted steel, volcanic stone, and weathered timber. As a result, Mexican houses have become more visually exciting and spatially sophisticated than ever before, without losing either the character or the simplicity that is the hallmark of a unique national signature. In the words of Marie-Pierre Colle, "A Mexican building, like a chorus of voices, sings a hymn of its heritage."

And what beautiful music it makes.

1

ORIGINS

The culture of modern Mexico is a rich tapestry of diverse influences. From the delicately ornate and impressively grand architecture of the Toltecs, Maya, and Aztecs, to the strong, pared-down Colonial style of the Franciscan friars, the architectural expression of today evokes a unique and eclectic past.

THE

HACIENDA

The hacienda was the first and most authentically Mexican building to emerge in the post-conquest era. As such it continues to exercise a powerful influence on the form that Mexican architecture takes today. The Colonial style and many of the features that distinguish contemporary architecture originated in these enormous country estates.

The hacienda was all about scale. Massive scale. These vast properties and the houses on them defy any conventional notion of a farm, or even a ranch. As Tim Street Porter points out in his book *Casa Mexicana*, "the haciendas were the landed estates of Mexico, some with territories as big as Belgium." They originated with land grants awarded by King Charles V to loyal conquistadors, but were often expanded by purchase of land or by seizures from Indians powerless to resist. This land grabbing was more a matter of prestige than practicality. Haciendas in some cases reached a scale far larger than was needed for agricultural output, indeed that was far too unwieldy to administer effectively. Isolated by their own magnitude, the haciendas had to be self-sufficient. They became communities unto themselves. The hacienda was church, store, hospital, school, and town hall for the population of *peóns* who worked its land, and the quality and extent of these facilities varied enormously from hacienda to hacienda, often according to the character of the *hacendado*.

The *hacendado* was an absolute master, the feudal lord of his own private fiefdom who profited enormously from the privileges of his position. A hacienda was a business—big business. Some generated income from a range of operations, but most specialized in the production of a particular commodity—whether it be sugar, grain, cattle, or tequila—often accumulating vast wealth. The ledger of the Cuervos hacienda, famous for its tequila, records that in the late 1900s the owners could count among their assets nearly three hundred horses and mules, over one hundred pairs of oxen, and four million blue agave plants grown on eleven separate properties. Hobby farms the haciendas certainly were not.

The money generated by these massive estates went in part to sustain the dilettante lifestyle of the *hacendado*, but it was also used to build houses on a scale as monumental as the surrounding lands were extensive. From a distance, some of the larger haciendas looked more like vast convents or cloisters than houses. One good

measure of this scale was their adjoining chapels, many of which were of a size and splendor that would certainly rival the most elaborate churches of Mexico's wealthiest towns. Such was the power, wealth, influence, and prestige that the haciendas had acquired by the early years of the 20th century.

But it was not to last. During the uprising of 1910, the People's Revolution, the haciendas became the targets of marauding gangs of *banditos* led by such legendary figures as Emiliano Zapata and Pancho Villa. Haciendas to the rebels were the embodiment of the vast gulf between the very rich and the very poor, in a country where seventy percent of all arable land was in the hands of just one percent of the population. Most haciendas were sacked, looted, and burned to the ground and a subsequent series of sweeping land reforms abolished the feudal hacienda system once and for all. The huge estates were broken up, their lands redistributed and the servile bonds that had tied *peón* to *hacendado* finally broken.

A number of haciendas, however, did escape the destruction. Situated outside the Colonial town of Querétaro, La Laja was then too small, and the area around it too poor, to attract the interest of Señors Zapata and Villa. But in the post-revolutionary period it has emerged as an important example of classic hacienda architecture. The origins of Mexico's Colonial style can easily be spotted in its imposing stone-paved courtyard, massive red walls, distinctive *ojo de buey* windows, imposing timber gates, and wrought-iron window bars. There is a certain nobility to La Laja that comes not from refinement but from proportion and volume. This can be seen in the impressive height of the ceilings, the incredible girth of the 16th-century columns supporting the patio overhang, the long, elegant tree-lined drive leading to the house, or the solidity of two-foot-thick walls. Even the age-old trees are of awe-inspiring dimensions. It is as if the horse, rather than man, was the frame of reference for the imposing dimensions of the house. As a result, everything from the structure to the furniture, down to the very candlesticks, seems too massive for humans.

PREVIOUS PAGE (16)

*The horse and the wall are symbols of Mexico's legendary haciendas. The bright red color of the wall is created by the traditional process of **almagré**, in which the local red clay is mixed with oil to produce a homemade paint which is continually reapplied.*

PREVIOUS PAGES (18–19)

The La Laja hacienda features a large, stone-paved courtyard, where the clatter of hooves is a constant reminder of Colonial times. The simplicity and vast proportions of the enclosing walls have had a powerful influence on Mexico's contemporary design.

OPPOSITE

A cobbled road leads up to the massive gates and imposing outer walls of La Laja. The shaded area conceals the entrance to the chapel of the hacienda, which lies to the right, while the door at the end of the courtyard leads to the kitchens.

But La Laja is more than a well-preserved vocabulary of historical architecture. Its clean, uncluttered lines and massive volumes continue to inspire contemporary architects, especially the Sordo Madaleno family, a second-generation dynasty of prominent Mexican architects. Juan Sordo Madaleno, a colleague of Luis Barragán, used his beloved La Laja as kind of architectural laboratory. The scale and proportions of his city projects were often based on lessons learned from the noble dimensions of his cherished estate. In the manner that Barragán explored and expressed ideas in his own house, so too was La Laja not just a source of inspiration to Juan Sordo Madaleno, but a private place to experiment with everything from furniture designs to the size and placement of walls.

After his death, his son Javier, also an architect, took over the estate. Like his father he spends most weekends and holidays at La Laja—he was even married in the hacienda's chapel. And although he is less likely to experiment with furniture, color, or decor—all of which his mother, Juan Sordo Madaleno's widow, is still actively in charge of—he too discovers architectural inspiration here. As he makes his rounds of the property, he is a keen observer of the roughly constructed walls of volcanic rubble, the fences assembled from twisted, time-weathered branches, and the play of light on wall surfaces that vary from rough and rugged to ageless polished patinas. And it is these textures that travel with him back to Mexico City to reappear in his urban designs.

But he is not the only architect in Mexico to be inspired by La Laja. In its clean lines, huge proportions, and impressive volume, a new generation of architects has discovered a layer of authentically Mexican ingredients to add to the nation's contemporary expression in architecture and design.

PREVIOUS PAGE (22)

For Juan Sordo Madaleno, La Laja was a source of inspiration and a canvas for experimenting with creative ideas. A square table seating sixteen takes pride of place in the dining room. A gold-leaf painting by Mathias Goeritz hangs on a massive Mexican-pink wall, while colored glass containers and church candles add ambience.

PREVIOUS PAGE (23)

Sunshine filtered through high **ojo de buey** *windows combines with candlelight to create a soft light in the chapel. An orange-painted wall provides the backdrop to the altar. The proportions of the chapel are exactly those of the hacienda* **granarias**, *which also inspired the interior proportions of the architecture of Luis Barragán.*

OPPOSITE

It's an outdoor life at La Laja. Most entertaining takes place under the long, overhanging roof of the patio. The massive columns, dating to the 16th century, have influenced an entire generation of Mexican architects, who have adopted their tremendous scale and simplicity in new domestic as well as commercial buildings.

CULTURAL

REVOLUCIÓN

"A ribbon around a bomb," was André Breton's evocative description of Frida Kahlo.

Kahlo's enormous *alegría* (spirit) was legendary. A celebrated artist in her own right, and wife of Diego Rivera, Mexico's best-known muralist, Kahlo has attained almost mythical status. She was a foremost personality in the artistic generation that stimulated and inspired the cultural renaissance of the 1920s and 1930s, and Casa Azul, her cobalt blue, fortress-like residence on Londres Street in Coyoacán, Mexico City, has become a symbol of the cultural awakening that followed a social and political revolution which had brought the *peón* or peasant to center stage.

Beautiful, willful, talented, and passionate about Mexican culture, Kahlo was the ultimate tragic heroine. Despite the pain and suffering caused by a horrible road accident at the age of eighteen, and the never-ending series of operations and complications that followed, she led the way to legitimizing a form of cultural expression that was previously considered unworthy of serious attention, namely the folk arts and crafts of Mexico.

The efforts of Frida Kahlo, Diego Rivera, Pedro Coronel, and Rufino Tamayo in art, and Jesús "Chucho" Reyes and Luis Barragán in design and architecture, changed the cultural profile of modern Mexico from a nation that copied and imitated to one that proudly celebrated its own folk crafts and traditions and the magnificent legacy of its pre-Hispanic civilizations. Before then, French architecture, French interiors, French decoration, French education, and French taste had defined the aspirations of the Mexican elite. All the most fashionable houses in Mexico City were built in the French style and the children of any self-respecting family that could afford it were educated in Paris.

This obsession with all things French can be partly attributed to Mexico's brief period of French rule from 1863 to 1867, under the hapless and inept leadership of Emperor Maximilian, an appointee of Napoleon III. But at a more fundamental level it betrayed a crisis of identity in a country still in the grip of European elitism—the powerful legacy of three hundred years of Spanish rule. Despite land reforms implemented by revolutionary leaders such as Emiliano Zapata and Pancho Villa, the movement towards creating a distinctly Mexican signature in the realms of art and culture did not really gain momentum until the 1920s.

The 1920s and 1930s were buoyant decades for Mexico, boosted by the discovery of oil and by the fact that Mexico escaped involvement in World War II. These years saw the convergence of the infectious energy, spirit, and conviction of an extremely talented group of individuals whose efforts and inspiration ignited a passion for Mexican traditions. The pre-Hispanic civilizations of the Toltecs, Olmecs, Maya, Zapotecs, and Aztecs were accorded a new respect and their art became as much an inspiration to this new breed of artist as African masks were to Picasso and the École de Paris. Diego Rivera was so passionate a collector of Mexican folk art that he was often teased by his contemporaries for buying it "by the kilo."

This was nothing short of a cultural revolution, and the house which Rivera and Kahlo shared in Coyoacán became its living symbol. Casa Azul was a treasure trove of Mexican folk art, decorated with candy-colored toys, small clay idols from Tlatilco, Mayan jades, obsidian blades, rock crystal monkeys, Kahlo's flower-embroidered Tehuantepec dresses, traditional pottery from Michoacán, village blown glass, folk jewelry, straw toys, large "fiesta figurines," Day of the Dead skeletons and Mexican masks. There were paintings by Rivera, landscapes by José María Velasco, and *retablos*, the naïve paintings that strongly influenced Kahlo's style. As in most peasant houses, the floor of the dining room was painted with bright yellow insect-repellent paint and the kitchen was tiled in traditional *azulejos*. The walls were hung with inexpensive painted pottery and even the garden, filled with exotic tropical foliage, featured ancient stone carvings and pre-Hispanic idols. Casa Azul was richly colorful and, above all, thoroughly Mexican. It was to have a profound effect on future generations of Mexican artists, designers, architects, and authors. Shortly after Kahlo's death in 1954, Rivera donated the house and all its contents to the Mexican state and Casa Azul became Museo Frida Kahlo.

In her brief, tragic, but powerfully emotive life, Kahlo's passion for Mexico's folk traditions helped steer this nation on to a path of self-discovery and indigenous pride.

PREVIOUS PAGE (26)

The studio which Rivera constructed for Kahlo as an annex to her family house, Casa Azul, was built in the same volcanic stone as the pyramids at Teotihuacán. It was adorned with terra-cotta pots for doves to nest in and recesses containing pre-Hispanic idols. The small clay figurines are from Metepec.

PREVIOUS PAGES (28–29)

Frida Kahlo spent her entire life in Casa Azul, named after **azul añil**, *the deep mat blue color traditionally used to ward off evil spirits in Mexican houses. All the outside-facing windows were filled in as a security measure to protect the exiled Trotsky, a house guest for two years, from Stalin's assassins.*

OPPOSITE

A pyramid, modeled on the Pyramid of the Sun at Teotihuacán, was built by Rivera in the garden of Casa Azul and used to display pre-Hispanic artifacts. The red-painted, stuccoed surface accurately reflects how the giant pyramids would have appeared when they were first discovered by the Aztecs.

CASA

BARRAGÁN

The name of Luis Barragán (1902–88) needs no introduction. He was one of the most influential architects of the 20th century, and although he only completed a relatively small number of projects in his lifetime (largely because he applied himself with great intensity to only one building at a time), his work is admired the world over.

Towards the end of his career, in 1980, Barragán was awarded the Pritzker Prize, the highest honor in architecture, and it was perhaps fitting that he received a sculpture by Henry Moore. Barragán was to architecture what Moore was to art: both men achieved the similarly elusive feat of distilling from a complicated wealth of influences the simplest and most powerful elemental forms.

Today, Luis Barragán is justly recognized as one of Mexico's most important artists, and to preserve his legacy his own house in the Mexico City neighborhood of Tacubaya has been converted into a unique museum. Not only is this house a manifesto of the creative principles that Barragán devoted his energies to refining, but it also bears witness to his day-to-day life. It functioned as office, studio, laboratory, library, and retreat; it was where he worked, sketched, meditated, and prayed, and it has been preserved virtually unchanged.

Barragán lamented the fact that words like "beauty," "serenity," "silence," and "magic" no longer form part of the modern architect's vocabulary. He designed not for the sake of architecture but for the sake of contemplation, opting for a sensual architecture and living his whole life with the unshakable conviction that "life deprived of beauty is not worthy of being called human."

Luis Barragán was born and raised in Guadalajara, and the memories of his time there never left him. The stony roads and bird-filled squares, ample houses, peaceful courtyards, and the solid-but-simple building tradition of his native state of Jalisco informed his lifetime's work. Perhaps because of this, it has become commonplace to suppose that his architecture evolved purely out of the vernacular of Mexico. This could hardly be further from the truth. Barragán's vision was inspired by a complex web of cultural influences that included Islamic art, the culture of Classical Greece, the metaphysical paintings of Giorgio de Chirico, the writings of Saint Teresa of Avila, the poems of Edgar Allan Poe, African art, Paul Gauguin's *Noa Noa*, the Balinese illustrations of Miguel Covarrubias, even David Hockney's swimming pools. His work

was driven not by nationalism but by an unceasing quest to achieve "an architecture of the senses and emotions."

This quest began when Barragán arrived in Paris in 1925, still only twenty-three years old. His first impression of the "city of light" was overwhelmingly negative. There seemed nothing in its cosmopolitan chaos that he could identify with. But gradually he formed affinities with Parisian cultural life. He became an admirer of Picasso, a fan of the Russian Ballet, an observer of Japanese art, and a student of Ferdinand Bac—literary man, architect, dandy, draftsman, and Barragán's mentor.

Barragán also traveled extensively in southern Spain and Morocco. He was captivated by the color, power, and beauty of the many-layered culture of the region. The Alhambra, in particular, secured a lifelong appreciation of Islamic architecture and art. But significantly, Barragán approached these worlds without relinquishing the thread that linked him to his origins and his own land. As Albert Ruy Sanchez observes: "Faced with the east and the Mediterranean, Luis Barragán was a lucid traveller who discovered, recognized, and admired. He was never that bewitched lover, prepared to turn the encounter into a new direction in life."

Ironically, it was his travels in the Mediterranean and Morocco and his extended stay in Paris that ultimately helped Barragán to see through the cultural confusion that reigned in Mexico. In one word—"Mediterranean"—Ferdinand Bac had shown him a way to redefine all the aspects of Mexico's architectural traditions that he instinctively loved, and in the process to grant them new legitimacy and authority. The haunting haciendas, with their vast contemplative spaces, pure lines, massive volumes, and elemental textures—all the ingredients he would later cultivate in his work—were now newly conceived by Barragán as Mediterranean.

The ludicrous grip of Francophilia was broken, replaced by possibilities that reached all the way to Tangiers, Venice, Istanbul, Alexandria, and Marrakesh. Everything previously dismissed as *ranchero* was now, in fact, Mediterranean—a simple shift in perception that represented a fundamental leap in the evolution of Mexican culture. Barragán would never look back.

PREVIOUS PAGE (32)

Casa Barragán is both a reflection of the man himself and a distillation of his ideas. In a quiet corner of the library, beneath a yellow painting by Mathias Goeritz, Luis Barragán would pray several times a day at a "minimal" altar.

PREVIOUS PAGES (34–35)

*Encouraged by his lifelong friend, the artist "Chucho" Reyes, Barragán arranged artifacts of everyday Mexican life in powerful still lives. Mirrored **pulquería** balls and terra-cotta **pulque** pots would become part of his distinct signature.*

OPPOSITE

*The scale, proportions, and geometry of the **granarias** of Colonial haciendas had a powerful influence on Barragán's work, as this view of the main living area of Casa Barragán makes clear. All of the furniture was of his own design.*

BEAM CEILING
SCREEN

1	2	3	4
5	6	7	8

PHOTOS IN ORDER OF
APPEARANCE – PREVIOUS PAGES (38–39)

1

Barragán disguised the transition between one space and another with elegant bladelike walls, using architecture as a screen to make the process of discovery of his house more tantalizing. Here, a yellow wall hides the second set of stairs leading to his bedroom.

2

The textures and colors, objects and materials of everyday life in Mexico were expressed by Barragán in his characteristically calm and refined manner.

3

The simple but powerful architectural device of painting one wall a bright shade of pink or yellow and the others white was a lasting signature of Luis Barragán's work.

4

This elegant cantilevered staircase is one of the most famous in modern architectural history. Its use of unpretentious material (pine timber) in a sculptural manner is pure Barragán. Its strength derives from the vertical beams embedded in the wall.

5

Virtually all of the furniture in the house was of Barragán's own design and often repeated his recurring theme of intersecting horizontal and vertical planes, as does this low storage unit in an upstairs reading room.

6

An arrangement of objects in a corner of Barragán's library exemplifies how he liked to experiment with the odd flash of bright color. Unframed photos, including one of himself, sit casually against a sloping vertical surface. In all details, his aversion to superfluous adornment comes through.

7

Light entering a space was a source of constant inspiration and invention for Barragán. Here, a series of hinged panels controls the amount and direction of light which enters: a simple idea with beautiful effect that was to influence urban architects the world over.

8

Barragán was one of the first contemporary architects to see the beauty of Mexico's indigenous black volcanic stone. He used it to pave the entrance area of Casa Barragán and to build this elegant sculptural staircase. The deliberate contrast between the black stone and the white wall creates a powerfully graphic effect.

OPPOSITE PAGE

The distinctive signatures of Barragán's work unite in the entrance to his home. On the wall hangs a gold-leaf painting by Mathias Goeritz; the wall facing the light is accented by bright Mexican pink; the floor and staircase are of local volcanic stone; and the writing desk is just a substantial timber slab cantilevered from the wall.

2

INTERIORS

There is something archetypal about the architectural forms created by Luis Barragán. His work embodies the Mexican soul and continues to inspire, influence, and inform Mexico's current generation of architects.

CONTEMPORARY

COLOR

Barragán was the first modern architect to introduce the colors of the Mexican market-place to his work. He translated the bright pinks, yellows, and purples of toys, fruit candies, candles, and clothes on to vast expanses of wall. Describing his approach, Barragán called color "a complement to architecture. It can be used to widen or enclose a space. It is also imperative for adding that touch of magic to an area...."

But all too common is the misconception that Barragán used color with wild abandon. People envisage his buildings as endless stretches of candy-colored pinks or bright yellows. In fact, Barragán gave much thought to the questions of which color to use and where to apply it. He would, he said, always begin by "imagining the wildest and most incredible colors." Then he would go back to his art books—to the Surrealists de Chirico, Balthus, and Delvaux, and to the work of his friend "Chucho" Reyes. "Page after page I observe the images and canvases until suddenly I spot some color I had previously imagined. Then I ask a painter to spread the colors on a large piece of cardboard and to place this against bare walls. I leave them there for several days and change them in contrast to the other walls. Finally, I decide on the color I like best."

Color was an element of Barragán's architecture which he used to give meaning to an area or to accentuate a space. As architect Ignacio Díaz Morales, also from Guadalajara and Barragán's lifelong friend, points out: "The most noted characteristic of Barragán's space is the use of color, which he never uses for picturesque effect, but architecturally to underline spatial expression." This approach to color is a lesson which the next generation of Mexican architects have made their own, and none more so than José de Yturbe. In his use of color, Yturbe is remarkably imaginative and vivid. He takes risks, and thereby pushes Mexican architecture forward, adding yet another layer of innovation to the distinct signatures of Mexican design.

The yellow courtyard, for instance, focal point of the library at one end and the living room at the other, features massive walls painted in the familiar bright yellow of Barragán's Casa Prieto. Yturbe, however, magnifies the intensity of this shade by placing it against a black volcanic-stone floor, which in turn is defined by a grid of bold white lines formed of chunks of marble. These contrasts increase the drama and impact of the courtyard space. And this, after all, was in Barragán's opinion the ultimate aim of architecture: to engage the senses and emotions.

Yturbe's experiments with intensity continue in the dining room, where he has used a bright blood-orange cotton to cover the walls. This warm, sensuous shade, despite its intensity, seems a complement to conviviality—appropriate for a space designed for eating and conversing. It is also specifically an interior color. Yellow, by contrast, is reserved for places where it can be set against the bright blue sky. Yturbe seems to use "contrast" and "intensity" by turns to create an impression. The entrance lobby is devoid of all color or decoration save a gold-leaf painting and an Assyrian pattern carved into the white stone floor. This is a quiet and soothing, white and neutral space. Only a yellow grid, illuminating the spiral staircase which winds its way down into the belly of the house, provides a faint hint of what is to come. Colorful spaces lead to colorless spaces which in turn lead to colorful spaces. Barragán always said that magic and surprise were his greatest inspirations. Here in Yturbe's house, magic is sustained throughout and each successive circular space brings new surprises.

Perhaps what is most revealing of Yturbe's approach to architecture is that he demolished his old house in order to build a new one, an act that reflects at once the approach of an artist and the mentality of a perfectionist. Barragán was renowned for changing his work midstream. He would make walls higher, lower, or eliminate them altogether. The work of construction was to him a creative process: "If a painter can completely modify his canvas," he reasoned, "an architect should be able to do the same with his work." Even in this respect, Yturbe has taken Barragán's approach one step further.

PREVIOUS PAGE (44)
*A ceremonial bowl from India filled with silver **pulquería** balls decorates a geometric opening to the courtyard of Casa Yturbe.*

PREVIOUS PAGES (46–47)
An impressive circular staircase leads from the entrance down to the main living areas, two stories below. The refined, white entrance hall features a gold-leaf painting on a massive timber cantilevered plinth and an Assyrian pattern carved into the white stone floor. The adjacent circular space is illuminated from above by a yellow-painted grid inspired by the pigeon coops of old haciendas.

OPPOSITE
The master bedroom, on the lowest floor of the house, is reached by a beautifully pared-down, geometric staircase. The yellow columns overhead are a contemporary interpretation of the massive overhead beams of Mexican Colonial architecture.

FOLLOWING PAGES (50–51)
The walls of the dining room are upholstered in the same blood-orange Mexican cotton as the tablecloth. The arrangement of silver plates and green apples on the wall leading to the kitchen was inspired by a trip to Vaux-le-Vicomte, a 17th-century château near Versailles.

FOLLOWING PAGES (52–53)
The double-height library is the main living and entertaining area. Antique family heirlooms punctuate the white-painted, strictly modern space. The red and gilded screen, commemorating a visit by the King's emissary, the viceroy, to New Spain, has been in the Yturbe family for three hundred years.

FOLLOWING PAGES (54–55)
The courtyard is of huge, black, volcanic-stone tiles, accented by seams of loose white marble chunks. The reflecting pool, defined by a continuous strip of rust-textured steel, dissects the courtyard on a diagonal.

SPLENDID

MAGNITUDE

"He liked large dimensions, magnificence, things splendid and conclusive. By magnitude I do not mean size. The work of Barragán was not prolific and it usually conformed to small format. One need only to view the paintings of Vermeer (no larger than 40 x 50 cm) to learn a revealing artistic lesson. Salvador Dali was once asked what he thought about muralism in Mexico. The artist responded with his characteristic sense of humor by saying that there was more art in the seamstress's needle painted by Vermeer than in all the gargantuan expanse of Mexican muralism."

This passage came from a piece written by Felipe Leal for *Artes de Mexico*, entitled "An Afternoon at the Home of Barragán." It was one of the last times Barragán was interviewed before his death in 1988, and Leal was fortunate to catch the maestro in a mood of meditative clarity. In the course of a long afternoon he was privy to reflections of great lucidity regarding Barragán's views of architecture, the influences on his life, and his impressions and disappointments.

Barragán's views on dimension or magnitude are especially interesting, for they anticipate a very contemporary approach to space. In order for a space to possess magnitude, Barragán believed, it was not essential that it be huge. Magnitude was an impression rather than a quantifiable fact. Any space, large or small, could be pared down to its essence and grandeur conferred by proportion and light. As in the approach of today's minimalists, atmosphere was to be evoked by architecture, not decoration.

According to those who knew him well, Barragán was uninterested in creating a "school" or in converting others to his ways of thinking; his was a very personal architecture, pursued for personal reasons. And yet his legacy has had an unparalleled role in shaping contemporary Mexican architecture. Barragán is accorded an extraordinary respect in today's Mexico. His house in Tacubaya, featured on pages 33–34, is a shrine for students and establishment alike. Throughout Mexico, particularly in Mexico City, newly completed projects bear witness to lessons learned from Barragán's buildings and from the insights he gained in a life dedicated to discovering "an architecture of the senses and emotions."

One house in the leafy Mexico City suburb of Las Lomas (literally, "the hills") is a particularly fine example of the influence of Barragán's ideas of "magnitude."

57

Although situated in an attractive tree-lined street, the designated plot was not ideal. Architect Manuel Mestre faced the challenge of a small, funnel-shaped site. His solution was to design a house that would follow this shape, converging to a narrow point at the back. He thereby created an impression of magnitude and made the gradual reduction in the width of the site hardly noticeable. The widest part of the house looks out on to a garden and fountain, while the narrow end overlooks a smaller, triangular-shaped garden. Thus, from anywhere in the interior, the house appears to be surrounded by greenery, though in fact it is not.

Inside, Mestre has also employed highly effective spatial illusions. Passageways with lower ceilings lead into rooms with very high walls, creating a sense of scale and of spaces opening out. The largest space in the house is the entrance hall, where a single, massive wall of blue accents the generous proportions and furthers the impression of "splendid magnitude." The sheer extravagance of light, space, and color of this centrally positioned reception area plays a large part in shaping one's general impression of the house, even though the other spaces are nowhere near as capacious. Mestre, like a magician, has created the illusion of space. Barragán himself was similarly fond of experimenting with illusion in his design. He liked to use "fake" walls to construct particular angles or lines of vision, and would frequently build models and endlessly rearrange the relationship of walls until he had achieved a desired effect.

In many cities these days in which space is at a premium, the practice of utilizing the entire site when building a new house is becoming increasingly commonplace. This is particularly true of Los Angeles. Yet often it results in the very opposite effect to that intended: the house ends up looking smaller, not bigger, than it really is. It is therefore a testament to Mestre's skill that he was able to fully utilize this site to create such an impression of magnitude.

PREVIOUS PAGE (56)
Geometric patches of pink and blue applied to this entrance façade testify both to the modern and the traditional characteristics of new domestic architecture. They also illustrate the strategic use of color in Mexican design, something often not appreciated. From the grandest to the most humble of buildings, color is used to highlight a particular wall or a certain detail to create maximum effect.

PREVIOUS PAGES (58–59)
Color, light, and shadow animate the entrance to a house designed by architect Manuel Mestre for clients in the exclusive Mexico City district of Las Lomas. Changing patterns are projected on to the walls by overhead timber beams inspired by the beams of traditional Colonial architecture. The imposing structure of weathered timber is a **trapiche***, a mill from an old sugar hacienda.*

OPPOSITE
In a corridor leading to the back of the house, the strict geometries of the space are once again punctuated by authentically Mexican features. Potted cacti; a **mesa chocolatera***, an old Colonial table for serving chocolate; and Mestre's signature rough-hewn beams (set below glass to allow the effect but not the weather) all introduce warmth and character to the interior architecture.*

DOOR

SERENE

GEOMETRY

On first impression, there is something both reassuringly familiar and spiritually empowering about this urban house in the Colonial district of San Angel in Mexico City. Its discreetly elegant spaces, noble proportions, and serene geometry evoke pure Barragán.

The predominant forms are cubic, expressed through a fusion of pre-Hispanic and Mediterranean traditions. The main ingredients, predictably, are the wall and the courtyard. But unlike most Barragán projects, the tall, silent walls that block out the chaos of the city are not painted vivid shades of magenta, yellow, or blue. Instead, the color scheme is beautifully muted—a great expanse of soft beige, highlighted by smaller accents of a deep rich brown. The resulting effect is exactly what the owners requested. This is an "urban" and an "urbane" house, a city residence that celebrates, rather than ignores, its location at the heart of the world's largest metropolis.

In an inspiring and modern manner, architect Andrés Casillas has brought Barragán's legacy up to date. And, in a sense, no one is more qualified to do so. Of all the projects Barragán completed in his lifetime, the one most frequently admired and published is the San Cristóbal estate of stables, houses, and surrounding grounds on the outskirts of Mexico City. Some high-profile contemporary architects rate it very highly indeed. The famous London minimalist Claudio Silvestrin, for example, goes so far as to say that San Cristóbal is the only building in the world that he truly admires. However, what is generally not appreciated about this famous pink-walled stud farm is that it was a collaborative project by Barragán and Andrés Casillas, also from Guadalajara. That this fact is not more widely known is largely due to Casillas himself—a serious architect, certainly, but not by today's publicity-hungry standards a serious ego. All his vanities, it would seem, are poured into his buildings.

To author Jorgé Esquince, "silence, repose, and contemplation are the elements of his signature… and light, water and stone are the letters of his alphabet." Esquince was in fact writing about Barragán, but the phrase applies equally well to this San Angel house conceived by Casillas. The walls, fountains, and trees of his design are infused with precise meaning, and the whole house is an exercise in "accuracy" and "truth." Casillas is described by Alfonso Alfaro as "a serious disciple of Barragán," and it shows.

All the lessons and opinions Barragán expressed or discussed during his lifetime are present, in an abstract or literal sense, in this remarkable building. There is an emphasis on beauty, in accordance with Barragán's guiding conviction that "beauty speaks like an oracle—and man has always heeded its message." Casillas exploits the power of the fountain, which Barragán believed "brings us peace, joy, and restful sensuality," and the garden, "in which the architect invites the partnership of the Kingdom of nature." And of course the house bears witness to the inspiration of "the unassuming architecture of the villages and provincial towns of Mexico."

Barragán passionately believed in the spiritual ingredients of architecture, qualities such as "Myth, Beauty, Silence, Solitude, Serenity, and Joy," and these are incorporated in a manner as skillful and sophisticated as in any project by Barragán himself. And yet Casillas, no less a perfectionist than his mentor, was ultimately dissatisfied with the house. Contrary to his wishes the clients decided to work on the interior spaces with the help of an interior designer. The Ortiz Monasterio family, owners of one of the most prestigious contemporary art galleries in Mexico, supplied a superb collection of modern Mexican art, which the interior designer combined with select antique pieces from China, England, and Italy, as well as a substantial assemblage of antique brass microscopes and measuring instruments.

But if the resulting interior is not how Casillas would have preferred, to the outsider the house offers captivating contrasts. The tension between the serenely geometric, coolly minimal outdoor spaces and the eclectic, art-filled interior sets up a successful dynamic. And despite Casillas's objections to the decorative interior, the focal point of the house remains the architecture. From all vantage points, the outdoor spaces of his design are always on view, and it is the beautifully refined courtyard in particular which dominates the spirit of the entire structure.

PREVIOUS PAGE (62)
A sculpture by Mexican artist Adolfo Riestra sets the tone for a sleek, sophisticated city house recently completed by architect Andrés Casillas in San Angel, an old Colonial quarter of Mexico City. Casillas's external palette of beige and brown creates an atmosphere of elegant restraint and urbane simplicity.

PREVIOUS PAGES (64–65)
A detail of a reflective pond testifies to the carefully considered, almost monastic spirit of the architecture of Andrés Casillas. Simple monochrome surfaces evoke the calm and serenity of Japanese gardens, but on a scale that in its massive proportions is thoroughly and unmistakably Mexican.

OPPOSITE
The subdued and urbane mood of Andrés Casillas's architecture is occasionally tempered by a characteristically Mexican burst of color. The outdoor entertaining area, paved in black volcanic stone and furnished with the ever-present Mexican equipal chairs, is painted a vivid shade of yellow.

1	2	3	4	5	6
7	8	9	10	11	12
13	14	15	16	17	18

PHOTOS IN ORDER OF
APPEARANCE – PREVIOUS PAGES (68–69)

1

The walls of Casa Ortiz Monasterio are clad in a coating of finely crushed marble, a refined version of a surface often used on larger public and commercial buildings in Mexico City.

2 & 12

Sculptures by Adolfo Riestra recall Mexico's pre-Hispanic past. One stands guard just outside the entrance, another in the deep blue entrance hall.

3

The stone stairs leading from the courtyard to the children's bedrooms were inspired by the staircase in the entrance of Luis Barragán's home (see page 41).

4 & 14

In the dining room, a pair of Chinese cupboards below a pair of silver-leaf mirrors introduce a pleasing symmetry.

5

A marble sundial inscribed with Hebrew script keeps track of the sun's movement through the courtyard during the day.

6, 7 & 10

The huge proportions of the artworks in the Ortiz Monasterios' collection complement the monumental scale of the architecture. The unusual painting by Rocío Maldonado in photo 6 is distinguished by the way the frame forms part of the work.

8 & 15

Spaces defined by overhanging horizontal walls are a feature that was also used to great effect in the San Cristóbal stables, a project which Casillas worked on with Barragán.

9

The cobalt blue entrance foyer, with its low ceilings and subdued lighting, contrasts with the soaring volume of the light-filled courtyard. The painting is by Miguel Castro Leñero.

11

The kitchen features a painting by Xavier de la Garza and a generous skylight above a small internal garden. Kitchens in Mexican houses, once strictly the domain of the domestic staff, have become spaces for informal meals and quick coffees.

13

A reflecting pool defines the outer boundaries of the house, enhancing privacy and creating a sense of space and serenity.

16

In contrast to the restrained architecture of the exterior and the courtyard, the interior has been painted in vivid shades of cobalt blue (left) and ocher.

17

A slender gap between two bladelike walls is a potent and poetic signature of Mexican architecture that has been imitated all over the world.

18

Modern Mexican art juxtaposed with European antiques: two ingredients that embody the eclectic mix of influences defining Mexican style today.

O**PPOSITE PAGE**

The fountain is another truly Mexican ingredient. This small reflecting pool constructed in black volcanic stone in a corner of the main courtyard spills evenly over all four sides, creating a subtly poetic effect.

FOLLOWING PAGES (72–73)

All of the interior areas interact with the calm, serene space of the courtyard. The only decoration is provided by two mature trees which were brought to the site and an installation of terracotta rings by contemporary Mexican artist Xawery Wolski.

FOLLOWING PAGES (74–75)

The walls of the reflecting pool in a quiet corner of this inwardly directed building provide the single burst of exterior color. Overhanging greenery from gardens behind the pool sides frames the soft Mexican blue walls and the sculpture by Gilberto Acevez Navarro.

LAS

PALAPAS

In the villages of Mexico's Pacific coast, architecture is closer to the earth. Fences are made of sticks; building is predominantly in wood and adobe (sun-dried mud bricks); and the *palapa* structure—a simple shelter roofed with a thatch of woven palm fronds—endures in a form little changed since pre-Hispanic times. "The isolation of the rural environment," observes Marie-Pierre Colle, "has produced a timeless vernacular architecture that...hardly needs any architects."

Even the powerful *Mexica* or Aztec Empire, which extended as far west as the Pacific, showed little interest in building along this coast as it did in the Valley of Mexico. Yet we know that Montezuma and other great rulers made regular pilgrimages here in search of sun, sea, and recuperation. Perhaps the extravagant beauty seduced the *Mexica* visitors into a state of euphoria, reducing their usual ambition to build great monuments in stone to a simple desire to enjoy the seductive surroundings.

Not much has changed. When it comes to building along Mexico's Pacific coast, a different set of rules applies. The monumental elements so prevalent in most contemporary Mexican architecture—the stone-paved courtyards and massive walls—are willingly discarded. In their place is a more dreamlike architecture that has no doors, no windows, and very few walls. Angles are replaced by sensuous curves, edges are more rounded, and furniture is forsaken in favor of built-in benches and beds.

In this landscape of palms, rainforest, and tropical humidity, architect José de Yturbe has built perhaps the ultimate escape. Nestled in the jungle, on a craggy peak overlooking the majestic Pacific coastline, he has erected a modern interpretation of the pavilions of wood and thatch that have been built along this coast for centuries. The house is not easy to find and even more difficult to reach. Four-wheel drive is essential. A red dirt road, which the rainy season turns to a slippery mud gully, winds its way past little farms and thatched huts almost as far as the beach, when a short pebble-paved pathway signals finally that this was the right road after all.

At first glance the house has all the appearance of some ancient temple long since abandoned to the ravages of the jungle—like an Angkor Wat on the coast. Massive faded-pink columns, covered by a canopy of green, are aligned like architectural sentries alongside a narrow stone path. Eventually one reaches an opening between two pillars framed by the strangling embrace of climbing *amates*, Mexican fig trees.

If the arrival seems a ritualistic experience, this is how it was designed to be. The house embodies what Yturbe calls the "ritual of transition." Behind the row of magnificent pillars one is immediately confronted by a vast space of "pebble paddies," organic-shaped tiers or steps, each carpeted with a layer of beach pebbles. Climbing these one finally arrives at the house, or rather the first of a colony of seven *palapas*, all designed for different needs and functions. The main *palapa* is an enormous structure, fifty feet high and fully eighty feet in diameter, situated on the highest part of the point and surrounded by uninterrupted views of the Pacific. Small winding paths paved with pebbles lead to the other pavilions. There is a dining *palapa*, several bedroom *palapas*, and two double-story *palapas* for children and friends.

Though some pavilions are almost overgrown by the ever-encroaching jungle, life at Casa las Palapas is hardly "roughing it." Each bedroom *palapa* accommodates a massive bathroom with a view of the ocean, and details such as electricity, overhead fans, and essential screen doors are all worked into the simplicity of each round structure. And despite the organic spirit of the design, Yturbe has not really abandoned the defining features of Mexican architecture—rather he has translated them into a Pacific vernacular. The stepped area leading to the *palapas* is a Pacific version of the courtyard, while the faded pink "sentry" pillars recall the wall that traditionally isolates private space from public.

Nestled in the verdant splendor of the Pacific jungle, Casa las Palapas allows one to enjoy the surrounding beauty free from 20th-century distractions.

PREVIOUS PAGE (76)
Massive pink cylinders flank the entrance to a house which at first glimpse is like stumbling upon an overgrown ruin lost in the jungle.

PREVIOUS PAGES (78–79)
*In defiance of the conventional idea of a house, Casa las Palapas consists of seven circular **palapas** or pavilions of varying size, each roofed with the traditional Mexican thatch of palm fronds and situated at different levels on an idyllic Pacific promontory.*

PREVIOUS PAGES (80–81)
*Sheltered from the sun by the low overhanging thatch, and open on all sides to the cooling sea breezes of the Pacific, there is no need for air conditioning, despite the tropical heat. The main **palapa** is an extraordinarily massive space—fifty feet at its highest point and a full eighty feet across. The monster proportions demanded an approach to the interior design that would not be overwhelmed by the huge scale, hence the division of the the main **palapa** into two different levels.*

OPPOSITE
*A stone-encrusted path leads from the main **palapa** to the dining **palapa**. Potted ferns and a still life of local shells, flowers, and banana fronds provide the simple decoration for this family retreat.*

FOLLOWING PAGES (84–85)
The decorative elements are inspired by the surroundings: massive conch shells carved from sandstone, copper pots filled with hibiscus flowers, and floor patterns created with pebbles from the shore below.

TACTILE

TEXTURE

Barragán's choice of materials, according to his friend and colleague Ignacio Díaz
Morales, was governed "by a sure sense of appropriateness…. His selection, although
often of humble materials, can yield most elegant results, not unlike that found in
countless small, simple ranches throughout the Mexican countryside. The textures
and qualities of Barragán's materials complete the harmony of his spaces."

The "humble materials" Barragán so often preferred have been staples of Mexican
architecture since long before the arrival of Cortés. Friar Bernadino de Sahagún's
detailed account of life in pre-Hispanic Mexico tells of legendary Toltec storehouses
filled with stone, timber, shells, and woven *petate* (palm) mats, while the eyewitness
testimony of Bernal Díaz describes stone palaces with elaborate timber beams, doors,
and screens, and internal feature walls of polished "greenstone." In the vast market-
place of the Aztec capital, Tenochtitlán, site of present-day Mexico City, timber beams
and planks had a special section. And Cortés discovered from tax rolls seized from the
defeated Aztecs that quantities of timber in specified shapes and sizes were a key com-
ponent of the regular tribute that the Aztec Empire exacted from conquered rivals.

Texture was an important feature of pre-Hispanic architecture. The stucco-
rendered façades of stone palaces were polished with river stones to a gleaming finish
that astounded the conquistadors. The privileged citizens of Tenochtitlán even
appointed officials whose sole task it was to maintain the pristine perfection of their
beautiful walls. The interiors of palaces were, by European standards, hardly furnished at all; texture played the dominant decorative role. Feature walls were covered
in some instances with thin sheets of gold, a precursor to the gold-leaf art of contemporary artist Mathias Goeritz (see page 41). Other walls were covered with brightly
colored cotton, like those of José de Yturbe's dining room (see pages 50–51). There
were also walls hung with extraordinary tapestries of vividly colored feathers or, in
the tradition of Teotihuacán, painted with elaborate fresco murals.

The Aztecs' admiration, indeed veneration, of the texture of natural materials is
shared by Mexico's current crop of contemporary architects. Javier Sordo Madaleno,
in particular, has a passion for texture. Constantly experimenting with inventive new
ways to employ the surface qualities of natural materials, he uses texture to accentuate a wall or space in the same way that Barragán used color. And he has introduced

weathered and rusted patinas to the creative equation of contemporary architecture, for unlike the perfection-driven Aztecs, he is fascinated by the *imperfections* of natural materials.

A house he recently designed for a retired couple in Neuva Vallarta, a modern marina community on the outskirts of Puerto Vallarta, is an inspiring example of his approach. A circular drive paved in chunks of volcanic stone leads to a massive staircase. The orange-painted, rectangular entrance space—in marine terms, a cove—features the rusted remains of an enormous marine buoy. Complete with a length of its original, massive mooring chain, this is at once a reminder of the seaside location of the house and an example of the inventiveness Javier Sordo brings to his passion for texture. As if to echo this marine marker, an even larger rusted "can" has been placed at the opposite end of the house in an identically shaped rectangular cove, this one painted blue. Barragán once declared that the two qualities which most inspired him were "magic" and "surprise." This house offers both in abundance.

Inside, a narrow, towering corridor that is at least the equivalent of three stories in height, illuminated by shafts of light entering through glass strips embedded in the ceiling, leads to a multi-tiered living space of dimensions that dwarf even its most substantial pieces of furniture. A dining table that seats eighteen shrinks into insignificance and a fan attached to the massive logs of the ceiling beams seems like a toy miniature in relation to the monumental dimensions of the space. More like a pavilion than a room, the space conjures up the experiences of the conquistadors when they first encountered the palace of Montezuma: "in this house there was a hall so vast that it would easily hold more than three thousand persons, and on the floor above there was a terrace where thirty horsemen could have run a tilt, as in a *plaza*."

Javier Sordo Madaleno grew up surrounded by the massive proportions of his father's hacienda La Laja. This house in Neuva Vallarta reveals how the magnificent dimensions of his childhood have become part of his adult architectural signature.

PREVIOUS PAGE (86)
Javier Sordo has utilized scale, color, and texture to dramatic effect in this coastal house. The orange entrance features an old and rusted marine marker buoy, complete with its massive mooring chain.

PREVIOUS PAGES (88–89)
The ancient stone temples of the Aztecs, Maya, Zapotecs, and

Toltecs are invoked by the stairs leading to the entrance of this contemporary home.

OPPOSITE
A central corridor of monumental proportions defines the main axis of this indoor–outdoor house. The living areas and smaller internal rooms all lead from the extraordinary triple-height space of this corridor.

FOLLOWING PAGES (92–93)
The main entertaining space, which functions like a covered courtyard, is divided into three separate areas. Another enormous marine buoy defines a blue-painted and tiled niche, which serves as a bar and impromptu kitchen. The seemingly endless staircase to the right leads to a bedroom and an observation room in a tower.

PAINTED
HEADERS
TILE PATTERN

MINIMAL

COLONIAL

On February 10, 1519, Captain Hernán Cortés and his eleven ships made landfall on the coast of the Gulf of Mexico. Within two years, the most powerful empire in all of Mesoamerica had been defeated by Cortés and the ragtag bunch of adventurers that accompanied him—just five hundred soldiers and one hundred sailors—concluding what must surely rank as one of the most extraordinary tales of conquest ever told.

Spurred on by the promise of gold and by a crusading zeal, Cortés marched his men across the mountains, into the Valley of Mexico, and onward to the Aztec capital of Tenochtitlán. There, in the middle of a lake, they encountered a spectacular city of massive pyramids, elaborate palaces, and vast marketplaces. It was, in the words of Bernal Díaz, chronicler of the conquest, "all so wonderful that I do not know how to describe the first glimpse of things never heard of, seen, or dreamed of before."

Less than two years later, in August 1521, the last Aztec emperor, Guatemoc, surrendered to Cortés in the "charred and desolate rubble" of what had once been "the brilliant capital of the largest empire in Mexico." And, as Richard Townsend, an expert on pre-Hispanic culture, explains: "even as the remains of Tenochtitlan were being razed to build colonial Mexico City, a group of Franciscan friars arrived at Cortés' request." Their mission as they saw it was the destruction of existing temples and idols, to be replaced as soon as possible by Catholic monasteries, cloisters, and churches. The speed with which they achieved this goal was truly astounding. Churches were built at a rate as high as one a week, and by the end of the 16th century almost all of the indigenous population had been baptized.

The style of the Franciscan missionaries was unmistakable. Pious, solemn, and devoted to a life without luxury or pretension, they built in a minimal manner. Ornamentation was frowned upon and their buildings were permitted the distinctions only of vast scale and classically inspired proportions. Colonnades, arches, and walls were at once the architecture and the decoration. It is no surprise then to learn that Barragán, also deeply religious, was strongly influenced by the Colonial architecture of these monks of Saint Francis. He admired the Franciscan philosophy of humility and austerity, and their faith in sobriety as a source of beauty. Many of the traits of their minimal architecture resurfaced in his own designs, as they also do in the work of Mexico's current generation of architects.

Franciscan minimal ideals contributed to architect Manuel Mestre's recent design for a house in Coyoacán, but he was also inspired by the 16th-century Colonial style of *plateresco*, the engaging if peculiar habit of building an elaborate baroque façade, but leaving the rest of the structure unadorned. Coyoacán, now a district of Mexico City but once the oldest Colonial city in Mexico, is distinguished by a collection of grand palaces and town houses, isolated from the streets by walled gardens.

One of these gardens was the site for Mestre's commission. The client had but one real stipulation: that the garden be kept intact. Not a tree was to be touched. The conventional Mexican theme of a massive house with a central courtyard had therefore to be abandoned. In its place Mestre designed a series of separate pavilions, breaking away from either side of a tall narrow wall that represents the *plateresco* baroque façade, and connected by stone-paved walkways. They somehow assemble themselves around the main part of the garden, whose focus, in a tradition dating back to the Islamic Moors as well as to pre-Hispanic Mexican civilizations, is the fountain.

The house is also constructed, in part, from the salvage of ruined convents and monasteries. The fountainhead was sculpted from a discarded block of Colonial stone and the stone archway that defines the front façade came from a convent in Puebla. Even the distinctive blue and terra-cotta color scheme has Colonial roots: it was inspired by the colors of La Conchita, an old convent in Coyoacán.

In the heat of Mexico's cultural renaissance during the 1930s and 1940s it was fashionable to depict the Spanish as the perpetrators of all evil, the ruthless destroyers of a priceless cultural legacy. Today that standpoint has mellowed somewhat. A new mood of pragmatism accepts that the extraordinarily exotic mix that is Mexican culture is such *because* of Mexico's history, not in spite of it. Colonial, as a result, is once again politically correct.

PREVIOUS PAGE (94)
*In the design of a house situated in the heart of Coyoacán, Mexico's oldest Colonial town, architect Manuel Mestre makes distinct reference to the 16th-century Spanish style of **plateresco**, in which all decoration other than a baroque façade was eschewed. The stone arch of the doorway was salvaged from a 17th-century convent in Puebla.*

PREVIOUS PAGES (96–97)
Set in a garden that once belonged to the famous Mexican actress Dolores Del Rio, the design of the house was determined by the present owner's wish to preserve all of the trees. With its distinctive red-and-blue color scheme and simple, almost monastic spaces, the house is a pared-down, contemporary version of Mexican Colonial architecture.

OPPOSITE
*The shape of the fountain was inspired by an **abrevadero de caballos** or long water trough at Chichimequillas, the hacienda where the architect grew up.*

FOLLOWING PAGES (100–101)
The fountainhead was sculpted from a single slab of stone by Mexican artist Curro Ulzurrum. It was a housewarming present from the architect to his client.

MODERN

MYTHOLOGY

Mythology and religion were central to Barragán's views on architecture. "It is impossible," he would argue, "to understand art and the glory of its history without arousing religious spirituality and its mythical roots that are the very *raison d'être* of the artistic phenomenon. Without one or the other there would be no Egyptian pyramids nor those of ancient Mexico." "Would," he asked, "the Greek temples and Gothic cathedrals have existed," or the "marvels of the Renaissance and the Baroque have been produced?" Would we, indeed, be the heirs to such an inexhaustible artistic treasury without mythology and religion?

Myth and legend have played a powerful role in the development of Mexican culture. Even today, pre-Hispanic cultures live on in the symbols, forms, and materials incorporated into modern art and architecture. In both an abstract and literal sense, houses, office buildings, hotels, sculpture, fountains, paintings, and monuments evoke the ancient mythology of Mexico's past.

Recent archaeological discoveries point to the fact that this is not just a modern-day phenomenon. Analysis of the legacy of the great *Mexica* or Aztec civilization has revealed that the Aztecs, too, invoked the past in their architecture and decoration, particularly the glories and achievements of their immediate cultural ancestors, the Toltecs. In comparing the archaeological remains at the Toltec city of Tula with discoveries at Aztec Tenochtitlán's Templo Mayor pyramid, it has become clear that more than five hundred years after the collapse of the Toltec empire, the Aztecs were adorning temples with the same imagery that the Toltecs had employed.

As Octavio Paz observes, art is the only legacy that lasts. It acts simultaneously as a reminder of past glories and a stimulant to better them. The mythology of Mexico provides a challenge to each new generation. Converting this legacy to the terms of everyday modern life is neither easy nor straightforward, yet it holds the key to a more meaningful and rewarding architecture.

Perhaps the most evocative example of a modern treatment of Mexican mythology and tradition is the house designed by architect Javier Sordo Madaleno for himself and his family in Mexico City. Here, one is made aware of the power of Mexico's past from the moment of approaching the gates. Beautifully simple and possessed of a very unusual patina, these gates appear at first glance to be very modern and unadorned.

But closer inspection reveals horizontal strips or beading of rusted metal, a detail that reflects the architect's interest in texture, but also the fact that metalworking was, and remains, one of the most important crafts in Mexico.

Inside the gates, the entrance hall—an open-roofed chamber with the atmosphere and dimensions of a meditation chamber in a Colonial convent—has as its only furniture a Colonial-period fountain carved from a single block of stone. This chamber leads to an impressive outdoor stone staircase, again lined majestically on either side by enormous pillars wrapped in Javier Sordo's signature rusted-steel rope. The stone steps lead down to the entrance of the house straight ahead and to a massive stone-paved courtyard to one side.

Mythical memories abound. The entrance to the house recalls the steps leading to the ruined palaces that line the Avenue of the Dead in the ancient city of Teotihuacán, while the stone courtyard with its high walls, one colored "Indian Red," mirrors the courtyards of pre-Hispanic temples. Even the azure blue pool, which seems to bring the house right back into the 20th century, evokes the many pools and baths mentioned in the first accounts of Montezuma's palaces. The Aztecs possessed a rich decorative sense, as the recollections of Bernal Díaz confirm: "The sight of the palaces in which they lodged us! They were spacious and well built, of magnificent stone, cedar wood, and the wood of other sweet smelling trees, with great rooms and courts, which were a wonderful sight, and all covered with awnings of woven cotton."

It is impossible to wander about Javier Sordo Madaleno's house without discovering spaces, objects, or textures that bring to life the mystique and beauty of some aspect of Mexican culture. This is a house in which modern living and Mexican mythology are inseparably intertwined. It confirms the truth of Edmundo O'Gorman's observation that: "The irrational logic harbored in myths and in all true religious experience has been the source of the artistic process of all times and in all places."

PREVIOUS PAGE (102)
Texture and scale provide the themes for architect Javier Sordo's own house in Mexico City. In the fountain court-yard, a calmly sculptural space, impressive height is combined with the serenity of running water and the natural texture of river stone.

PREVIOUS PAGES (104–105)
Pre-Hispanic idols, displayed here in a specially constructed alcove, have been a staple decorative ingredient of the Mexican home since the cultural renais-sance of the 1920s and 1930s. The paint finish of these pieces is a hand-applied effect, similar to sponging.

OPPOSITE
The soaring height of the entrance lobby is revealed by the tree in the garden, which is cleverly framed by a long, nar-row glass panel. The floor is of stone inset with weathered tim-ber, and the scale of the space is complemented by the huge pro-portions of the furniture.

1	2	3	4
5	6	7	8
9	10	11	12
13	14	15	16

PHOTOS IN ORDER OF
APPEARANCE – PREVIOUS PAGES (108–109)

1

The entrance foyer of Javier Sordo's Mexico City home is illuminated by an overhead grid open to the sky. Shafts of light fall on to a floor formed of chunks of volcanic stone inlaid with panels of rusted steel.

2 & 14

The sunken stone courtyard at the front of the house was built using a centuries-old stonecraft technique. The walls of the adjacent entrance foyer are painted "Indian red," a popular color in pre-Hispanic times.

3

An internal corridor is illuminated from above by a long, narrow skylight and features an iron latticework gate modeled on the woven bamboo doors often found in the simple dwellings of rural Mexico.

4 & 13

The red dining room combines baroque Colonial candelabra, a silver-framed painting by Rosario Guerrero from Oaxaca, and Javier Sordo's simple, massively constructed furniture.

5

A polished stone staircase leading to the children's bedrooms is highlighted by a single shaft of white light created by a long narrow slit in the ceiling over the double-height stairwell.

6

Steel cable laid horizontally on a feature wall generates a highly unusual effect in the living room: despite its ruggedness, the impression is of high sophistication.

7

A double-height alcove provides the space for still lives of dramatic proportions. The arrangements reflect the seasons: in this case, bundles of dried wheat signify that it is harvest time.

8

The lap pool runs the entire width of the courtyard and is connected by an underwater passage with the shower area in the master bathroom. Early Spanish descriptions of Aztec palaces always mentioned elaborate outdoor bathing pools.

9

Highlighted by a splash of color in an interior dominated by neutral tones, this cutout in a wall of the dining room features a sculpture by Manuel Fuentes and a painting by Francisco Toledo of Oaxaca.

10

Mythology and tradition are evoked by even the smallest details. The candelabra in the dining room are suspended from metal chains—a reminder of the long history of the craft of metallurgy in Mexico.

11

The master bathroom, larger than many small urban apartments, overlooks the stone courtyard at the front of the house. Once again, neutral tones and the textures of stone and timber predominate.

12

Light, color, scale, texture, and mythology define this house. A statue of a pre-Hispanic deity sits on a massive chest of drawers in the main entrance hall.

15

With the sun directly overhead, one of Javier Sordo's signature long, narrow skylights casts a strip of sunshine on to a striking pink-and-blue Turkish kilim in the entrance hall.

16

The stairway leading from the entrance lobby to the main body of the house is flanked by massive pillars. Their surface of rusted steel cord recalls the rope lashing used in pre-Hispanic construction.

O PPOSITE PAGE

The ornate detailing of an antique Venetian bureau contrasts well with the unusual texture of a feature wall laid with horizontal steel cord in the living room of architect Javier Sordo's Mexico City home, depicted in photo 6.

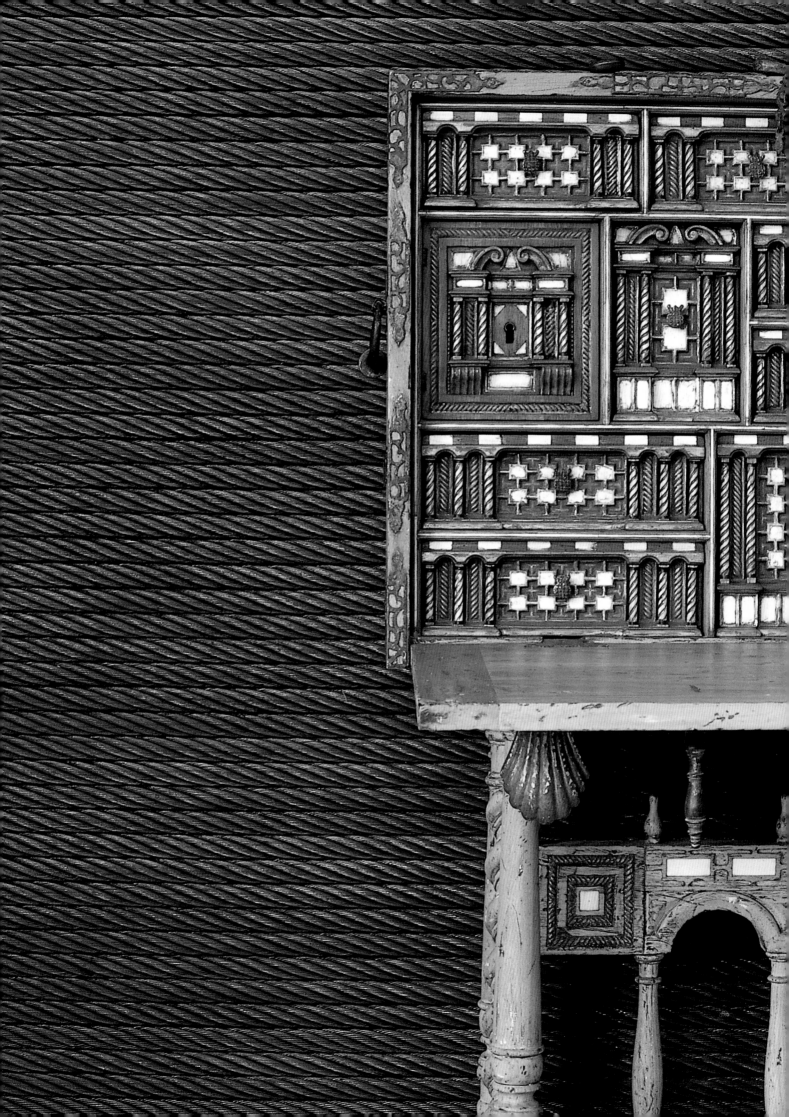

3

COLORS

*Strong color is the hallmark of Mexico. Vibrant blues, bright yellows, and the ubiquitous **rosa mexicana** (Mexican pink) distinguish not only the intersecting planes of sophisticated urban architecture, but the buildings of rural villages and the very ingredients of everyday life.*

COLOR

FIESTA

Color, in the words of Marie-Pierre Colle, is "the essence of the Mexican spirit."

The Aztecs, the Maya, the Toltecs, and the Zapotecs all had a love of elaborate decoration and bright color. In a passage from his classic memoirs, *The True History of the Conquest of New Spain*, Bernal Díaz recounts the first time the Spaniards witnessed the dazzling panoply of Aztec royalty: "Cacamatzin the great lord of Texcoco, a nephew of the mighty Montezuma arrived with greater splendour than we had ever beheld in any Mexican prince. He came born on a litter, most richly worked in green feathers with much silver decoration and precious stones set in tree designs that were worked in the finest gold...." And as the conquistadors discovered upon entering Tenochtitlán, the Aztecs' rich decorative sense was also expressed in their houses, palaces, and gardens.

Díaz's elaborate descriptions did not often make reference to the specific colors of the Aztec Empire, but the evidence of archaeology, thankfully, is much more revealing. Comparative studies indicate that the colors favored by the Aztecs in their architecture were also those of the earlier Toltec civilization. The images carved into the benches lining the walls of the "Hall of Eagle Warriors" in the Templo Mayor pyramid of Tenochtitlán, and the rich colors used to paint them, are *Mexica* or Aztec recreations of similar benches in the Toltec city of Tula, which had brilliant red backgrounds, plumes and body ornaments painted bright cerulean blue and yellow, and outlines in black. Both Toltec and Aztec artists used an orange-tan color to depict skin tone—a shade which, in an original and unexpected reworking of an ancient artistic convention, architect José de Yturbe has used extensively in recent projects.

An even greater and more monumental testament to the Mexican love of color is the ancient city of Teotihuacán (200 BC–AD 750), site of the Pyramids of the Sun and the Moon. It is difficult to imagine today, looking at these enormous piles of volcanic stone, that they were once covered by a ten-inch-thick layer of smooth stucco, and that each pyramid was a single, dominant color. (The evidence of surviving patches of color-impregnated stucco suggests that the Pyramid of the Sun was red and the Pyramid of the Moon ocher.) Small surviving fragments also reveal that the surfaces of the pyramids, like the cathedral ceilings of Europe, were decorated with vast frescoes depicting hunting scenes, sacred animals, and religious rites. What a sight it must

have been when the Aztecs first discovered this abandoned city. The pyramids were so beautifully finished that the Aztecs were long convinced that each structure was, indeed, a monolith, carved by giants or gods from a single chunk of brightly colored stone. And even modern scholars are still not clear which Mesoamerican people built Teotihuacán.

Today, there is no lack of evidence to confirm that Mexico has always been a colorful country, but colorful has not always been fashionable. Mexico's entry early this century into the modern world brought with it, as in other nations, a trend towards the International Style in architecture. This was an architecture of clean lines, hard-edged materials, and little, if any, color. It was, nonetheless, what the best-dressed cities were wearing and for a while Mexico, particularly Mexico City, followed suit.

It took the rare creative energies of a group of extremely talented artists to guide Mexico's urban expression back to truer native traditions. Leading this movement were Diego Rivera with his murals, Frida Kahlo's patronage of popular Mexican arts and crafts, Rufino Tamayo's paintings, and of course Barragán's massive expanses of solid pink, yellow, and blue.

Although Barragán was truly the master of color as an architectural tool, the idea of introducing these quintessentially Mexican colors came from his close friend and collaborator, Jesús "Chucho" Reyes. Reyes was an artist of eclectic talent: an antiquarian, painter, decorator, and "inexhaustible source of ideas." He was an enthusiastic spokesman for Mexico's indigenous cultures and encouraged Barragán to look to the colors of the sweets, fruits, and toys on display in the Mexican marketplace and to experiment with expressing this popular palette in unexpectedly urban and urbane ways. Today, great expanses of pink, yellow, and blue have become a ubiquitous display of pride in the indigenous traditions of the Mexican nation.

PREVIOUS PAGE (114)
At Las Alamandas, a small, idyllic retreat on the Pacific coast, a blue alcove is illuminated from an open skylight, providing the perfect backdrop for a luscious sago palm.

PREVIOUS PAGES (116–117)
Stone stairs have defined Mexican architecture since the very earliest Mesoamerican civilizations. This staircase leading to one of the villas at Las Alamandas, designed by Isabel Goldsmith, incorporates all of the vibrant colors of Mexico.

OPPOSITE
Color at Las Alamandas is used as an architectural code. Each villa has a strong bias towards yellow, pink, or blue and is named accordingly: Casa del Sol, for example, is yellow.

FOLLOWING PAGES (120–121)
Of all the colors of Mexico, the most alluring is pink, particularly here, where it is partially hidden by the verdant green of sweeping palms at the Westin Regina Pacific resort hotel, a joint project by architects Javier Sordo and José de Yturbe.

FOLLOWING PAGES (122–123)
The combination of pink and yellow recurs everywhere in Mexico, as here in a still life of sunflowers and bougainvillaea petals on the dining table in the house of architect Javier Sordo.

FOLLOWING PAGE (124)
The patina of age and the vitality of color are what make the walls and buildings of Mexican villages so seductive. A weathered blue wall in Cholula mimics the pattern made by sunlight and shadow at Las Alamandas on page 114.

"My roots are in Mexico; I had the good fortune to live in the countryside, in small villages…. When I use a strong color like red or purple, it is because my mind has suddenly been illuminated by the memory of some Mexican festival, some stall in some market, the brilliance of a fruit, a watermelon or a wooden horse…. In Mexico people invent colors; in Pátzcuaro there are pinks and reds; Huejotzingo also has marvellous colors— indigo blue, plaster white—this is timeless architecture which will never outlive its period because it belongs to no period…."

Luis Barragán, interviewed in 1976 by Elena Poniatowska, quoted by Mariana Yampolsky in *The Traditional Architecture of Mexico*

4

INGREDIENTS

A wealth of craft traditions provides the ingredients of Mexican culture. Since long before the arrival of the Spanish, Mexican artisans have been making exquisite objects in clay, silver, and cloth. And to this day, their work continues to adorn the Mexican home.

TIN-GLAZED

TILES

In Colonial times the most important center for the manufacture of tin-glazed earthenware was the city of Puebla, founded by Cortés. Today, throughout this historic town and its surrounding areas, the decorated façades of 17th- and 18th-century churches and houses stand as evidence of a tradition which still thrives.

These magnificently gleaming façades embody Mexico's rich and far-reaching cultural heritage: *azulejos*, or glazed tiles, were introduced to Mexico by the Spanish, who had learned the technique of glazing from the Moors of southern Spain; the Arabs had inherited the craft from the Persians, who had themselves learned it from the Chinese. Before the arrival of the Spanish, pottery-making in Mexico was limited to unglazed earthenware fired at relatively low heat. It is little wonder then that the local artisans were mesmerized by the bright colors and impervious shiny finish made possible by the technique of glazing.

Tin glazing in Mexico is called *talavera*, after the town of Talavera de la Reina in Spain, where similar tin-glazed pottery was traditionally produced. With time *talavera* has also become a generic term for all Mexican glazed ceramics. The secret to glazing lay in the temperature of the kiln and in the double firing process. A combination of two types of clay was used to make the tiles. Once the clay had been mixed, soaked, and worked into medallion shapes, these were painted with a thin coating of a white glaze made from tin and some white lead and fired at a moderate temperature. These "soft fired" tiles were then decorated in floral or geometric patterns before being returned to the kiln to be fired a second time at a much higher temperature (2000°F). During this stage the oxide pigments literally melted into the glaze to produce the traditional bright colors of *azulejos*.

Today, perhaps the best example of the craft of *azulejos* can be seen in two *pueblitas*, or little villages, on the outskirts of Cholula. Here, not more than half a mile apart, are the extraordinary churches of Santa Maria Tonatzintla and San Francisco Acatepec. Elaborately decorated with tiles made in nearby Puebla, the frenetically colorful façades of these structures evoke the exotic styles of the Aztecs and Maya far more than the somber mood of a Catholic church. Christian saints are depicted swaddled in the feathers of the quetzal bird, their faces protruding from headdresses of corn leaves, in exactly the manner that pre-Christian deities were represented.

The style of these churches is described as Indian Baroque, because the indigenous Mexicans who were enlisted by Catholic missionaries to build them used pre-Hispanic concepts and motifs to present Christian scenes. They reflect the joyful sense of color and craft possessed by the civilizations that predated the Spanish conquest. Luckily, this Mexican love of decorative pageantry proved resilient enough to survive the devastations inflicted by the Catholic conquistadors.

One of the principal concerns of the Spanish conquerors was to lay hands on as much gold and silver as possible to fund the myriad religious wars King Charles V was waging in Europe. But they were also intent on converting the population of Mexico to Christianity as rapidly as possible. Horrified by the then regular occurrence of human sacrifice and the even less appealing practice of feasting on the cooked limbs of the victims, the Spanish sent a virtual army of missionaries to New Spain.

The business of the church was to build, and build they did. Today, even the smallest *pueblita* often boasts half a dozen churches. This feat of construction would have been impossible without the labor of the local population. The Spanish missionaries, adept at achieving God's work, helped to win over the native Mexicans by allowing their input and expression in the decoration. The indigenous people in turn were clearly fascinated by the newly introduced method of tin glazing. Their enthusiasm is communicated in the sheer exuberance of these Indian Baroque façades.

The old art of *talavera* is still practiced in Puebla using methods and materials that have scarcely changed since the 16th century. The handmade, imperfect quality of tin-glazed tiles has not only made them a popular item for export, but they also continue to be a part of the decorative expression of Mexican buildings. Simple, diagonal-patterned, blue-and-white *azulejos* can be found in restaurants and hotels, as well as in contemporary kitchens, bathrooms, courtyards, and swimming pools.

PREVIOUS PAGE (128)
The church of San Francisco in Acatepec is an example of Indian Baroque style, so-called because it represents the indigenous Mexicans' interpretations of Catholic myths. The incredible decoration of this façade owes to the proximity of Puebla, tile-making capital of Mexico, and the missionaries' eagerness to involve their new converts with the church.

PREVIOUS PAGES (130–131)
Of all the patterns and colors of Mexican tiles, the most visually striking and modern in spirit (although it is in fact hundreds of years old) is the simple blue-and-white diagonal pattern known as **talavera** *(also the generic term for glazed ceramics).* **Talavera** *tiles lend themselves to the creation of impressive geometric patterns, as here on a church dome in Puebla.*

OPPOSITE
Ranging from downright gaudy to remarkably simple and restrained, the Colonial façades in the historic town of Puebla display an extraordinary variety of colors and patterns. Whether a building was originally private or municipal, religious or secular, its tiled façade can speak volumes about the personality, taste, wealth, and status of the former owner.

CREATIVE
CLAY

"On reaching the market-place, escorted by the many *Caciques* [chieftains] whom Montezuma had assigned to us, we were astounded at the great number of people and the quantities of the merchandise, and at the orderliness and good arrangements that prevailed, for we had never seen such a thing before…. Every kind of merchandise was kept separate and had its fixed place marked for it…. [There was] pottery of all kinds, from big water jars to little jugs, displayed in its own place."

Bernal Díaz's recollection of his first visit to the Aztec marketplace of Tenochtitlán, recorded in his fascinating memoirs, *The True History of the Conquest of New Spain*, is the first European testament to the importance of the art of pottery in this ancient culture. Yet in fact the most spectacular ceramic pieces produced by Aztec artisans never made it to the markets. Instead, they were reserved for temples. These ritual ceramics were often adorned with the figures of deities or the ritual dancers of Aztec religious ceremonies, in all their spectacular and colorful costumes. Because the Aztecs had not discovered the process of kiln-fired glazing, however, most surviving pottery has long since lost its colorful decoration.

The typical pottery of Aztec day-to-day life in the 15th century was often red- or cream-colored and decorated with fine geometric lines with a calligraphic quality, or with natural motifs of fish, flowers, or animals. The finest examples of functional pottery were produced in the town of Cholula, situated on the outskirts of the city of Puebla. Indeed, the distinctive red-and-black ware of Cholula was the personal favorite of Montezuma. Formerly Cholollan, this Indian town was one of the first victims of Cortés's forces, but it has managed to keep its preeminent position in the art of pottery throughout Mexico's turbulent post-conquest history.

The sheer quantity of clay vessels and figurines made in the Valley of Mexico was extraordinary. A small insight into the scale of pottery manufacture at the height of the Aztec Empire is provided by Bernal Díaz's observations of a typical meal taken by the emperor Montezuma: "As soon as the great Montezuma had dined, all the guards and many more of his household servants ate in their turn. I think more than a thousand plates of food must have been brought in for them, and more than two thousand jugs of chocolate…." The earthenware needs of Montezuma's household alone were evidently huge. Given that the population of Tenochtitlán in the late 15th century was

approaching three hundred thousand (at a time when Spain's capital city Castile had less than twenty thousand inhabitants), the immensity of this craft industry becomes clear. And we should remember that all pre-Hispanic ceramics were produced without the pottery wheel, which was not introduced until the arrival of the Spanish. Pots, urns, jugs, and bowls were made by coiling strips of clay and then scraping and "paddling" the vessel to smooth and thin its walls.

Interestingly, not much has changed. According to Chloë Sayer, author of *Arts and Crafts of Mexico*, "Mexico is still a nation of potters." And in rural areas today, pots and pans continue to be produced by the technique of hand-coiling, just as they have been for centuries. In the cities, however, the taste for pottery has shifted to reflect a greater concern with the *art* of pottery. Pre-Hispanic ceramics are highly prized and eagerly collected, especially ritual ceramics, but so too is new work distinguished by the signature or style of an individual artisan. One particularly successful example is the pottery of Gorki González of Guanajuato. Using methods employed three or four centuries ago by the Spanish and Portuguese, he makes fine maiolica dinnerware decorated with original patterns inspired by both Mexico's Colonial heritage and pre-Hispanic traditions (see photo on page 158).

Countless other examples attest to Mexico's current creativity in clay. The nation's pottery is as diverse and emotive as the land itself. It is much to the credit of the Mexican people that through their patronage they actively encourage the development of the potter's craft, recognizing that this powerful tradition is another facet of Mexican culture which needs to be simultaneously preserved and reinvented. But above all, as Chloë Sayer writes, "the pottery crafts of Mexico have one thing in common: functional, ceremonial or purely decorative, all are worked with charm...."

PREVIOUS PAGE (134)

The large terra-cotta pot has become a definitive ingredient of Mexican architecture and design. Encouraged by his friend "Chucho" Reyes to introduce the traditional arts and crafts of Mexico to his work, architect Luis Barragán became well known for his simple groupings of terra-cotta pots (see page 35). Today, clay pots old and new are often arranged as still lives, particularly in the corners of courtyards.

PREVIOUS PAGES (136-137)

Less than a century ago, only French styles were deemed acceptable by Mexico's cultural elite. The craft of the village potter was considered too crude to be taken seriously. Today, thanks to the cultural revolution that began in the 1920s, Mexican naïve pottery is highly prized. The dining room of a contemporary home in Neuva Vallarta (see pages 86–93) gives pride of place to a collection of clay vessels and figures.

OPPOSITE

Terra-cotta idols were the most beautifully crafted examples of pre-Hispanic pottery and as such are now very much in demand. So much digging goes on in Mexico that new examples are found every day, and although the chances of finding a piece with as much character as this decorative jug are slim, centuries-old pots and idols produced by the Aztecs, Maya, Toltecs, and Zapotecs are still being discovered.

5

VIRTUOSI

The contemporary architecture of Mexico is distinguished by a sense of honesty. It is true to the traditions, temperament, and character of the nation. The strikingly modern yet distinctly Mexican creations of today evoke the powerful legacies of Mexico's pre-Hispanic era and the styles of her Colonial past.

MEXICO

MODERNO

"Modern but not Modernist" is how the writer Octavio Paz once described the work of Luis Barragán.

The same could be said of architect José de Yturbe. Of the present generation of Mexican architects, his work is probably closest to the ideals set by Barragán. Yturbe makes use of the same palette of bright color, and most of his work features the high walls and silent courtyards that Barragán was also fond of. But above all, his and Barragán's buildings are profoundly similar in spirit.

Yturbe's architecture is concerned with the notion of transition. He likes to create areas and spaces, often of spectacular color and proportion, that serve no other purpose than to lead to other spaces. This "ritual of transition" is perhaps too poetic a concept—too much of a waste of space—for the practical mind of the Westerner, but it has played a part in Eastern cultures for centuries. In the age-old palaces of India and the ancient temples of Japan, great attention was paid to the ritual of entry. Gates, corridors, archways, and courtyards were orchestrated in sequence in order to build a sense of anticipation. The resulting journey of discovery emphasized the importance both of the building and the reason for visiting it.

This same orchestration of spaces is at the core of Yturbe's architecture. It is an approach that stimulates intrigue, curiosity, mystery, and surprise. In short it represents the "architecture of the emotions and senses" which in Barragán's eyes was the ideal and the ultimate.

Yturbe's design for a golf club in the picturesque valley of Malinalco is a fine example of how this "ritual of transition" can work for a commercial building. Surrounded by volcanic peaks and blessed with an ideal climate, Malinalco, an hour-and-a-half's drive from the bustle of Mexico City, seems an ideal location for a golf course. But that is where any reference to the standard idea of a golf club ends. Approached by a winding road paved in black volcanic stone and lined with cacti of monumental proportions, the façade of the clubhouse is a monolithic slab of orange, punctuated by a single geometric cutout—a dark square on an otherwise unbroken expanse of wall. This entrance, made even more dramatic by the extraordinary thickness of the wall, leads to an enormous courtyard which is sheltered on four edges by an overhanging roof and open to the sky in the middle.

In the center of the court, beneath the sky, sits a massive round fountain that is as Zen as anything one might find in Japan. A single ball of stone emits a stream of water, creating a never-ending sequence of concentric circles which travel towards the edge of a circular stone. A visiting Japanese architect commented that it was "the most perfect silence" he had ever seen. But the visual impact of this courtyard is not limited to the fountain. Along one side is a strong and colorful reference to the pre-Hispanic fascination with steps: tiers of pink horizontal planes, decorated with a symmetrical sequence of massive potted geraniums, cascade like a waterfall into the space of the courtyard.

And what is the function of this space? None. It exists purely to create an experience, a pleasure which enhances the ritual of entry and makes the journey to other spaces more meaningful. There is a poetry to this kind of approach that is lacking in most of the "function first" architecture of the western world. Yturbe uses the Japanese concept of *wabi* when he is trying to give words to his approach to design. *Wabi* is the Zen notion of "voluntary poverty," a spirit achieved when something cannot be reduced any further—when it is as pure as it can be. This process of reduction or distillation, a continual striving to reach the essence, is not new to the art world. The sculpture of Henry Moore and Constantin Brancusi has *wabi*. But it was Luis Barragán who was probably the first modern architect whose work achieved *wabi*. Nothing could be removed to make it better. It was reduced to its essence.

Yturbe strives to achieve the same in his architecture. A recent expression of this quest is his own house in Mexico City. In the entrance to this house, the "ritual of transition" and the concept of *wabi* meet. A windowless expanse of wall and massive rusted steel doors give nothing away to first impressions. Behind the door one finds oneself in a narrow channel, defined by two towering yellow walls and paved in black

PREVIOUS PAGE (142)

Architect José de Yturbe believes in "the experience of architecture." He often creates spaces whose sole purpose is to lead to other spaces. In this recently completed house in Mexico City, the visitor enters via a slender gap between two tall, brightly painted walls. Rusted steel pots and a floor of broken pieces of black volcanic stone complete the picture.

PREVIOUS PAGES (144–145)

On passing through the opening depicted on page 142, the visitor immediately encounters the first courtyard, an enormous, sky-bound space, painted bright yellow and orange and featuring row upon row of majestic blue agave plants. It recalls both the stairs and steps of pre-Hispanic architecture and the agave fields around the old town of Tequila.

OPPOSITE AND FOLLOWING PAGES (148–149)

The second courtyard is a reminder of the strong influence of the fountain in Mexican architecture and design. The shapes are once more reminiscent of pre-Hispanic temples, while the color is as bright as it could be. Texture is introduced in the rusted steel which defines the edge of the pool and in the black volcanic stone floor.

volcanic stone. Like an open-topped tunnel, this passageway leads to a long slender gap in one of the walls. Passing through, one emerges into an open courtyard—a huge, impossibly bright space of yellow and orange steps climbing to the sky. These horizontal tiers of color are planted with endless symmetrical rows of large, identical specimens of blue agave, the cactus from which tequila and mescal are distilled. The courtyard is charged with the pure spirit of Mexico. After the narrow confines of the initial passageway its effect is spellbinding. Yet the ingredients are simplicity itself. Walls, color, plants, and steps—nothing more. It is infused with *wabi*.

And the ritual of transition doesn't end here. The courtyard is only one element in an orchestration of visual experiences, captured on pages 142–156. But though we might applaud the poetry and spirit of Yturbe's approach, there is a question that lingers unanswered: is this elitist? Certainly, the golf club at Malinalco was possible only because the wealthy client could afford to incorporate the experience of transition. But perhaps the skeptical should look to the resort in Puerto Vallarta designed by Yturbe in collaboration with his former partner Javier Sordo Madaleno for the Westin Group. This mammoth complex contains more than five hundred rooms, countless apartments, an entertainment complex, a shopping arcade, and a handful of restaurants. With no pretension to being anything else, it represents a full-tilt assault on the foreign tourism dollar. German, Dutch, Japanese, and American tourists arrive by the organized bus-load. And these are not select architecture tours; their members are more intent on sampling sun and tequila than discovering Mexican design. Yet few fail to be impressed by the architecture surrounding them. Even to the untutored eye, the colors, scales, and textures of the resort are mesmerizing. And this, after all, was Luis Barragán's greatest aspiration: to create architecture that appealed directly to the emotions and the senses.

OPPOSITE
The bold shapes and colors of pre-Hispanic civilizations are strongly evoked by the high rise architecture of this resort hotel in Puerto Vallarta, which demonstrates the growing ease with which contemporary architects such as José de Yturbe are able to infuse large-scale commercial buildings with distinctly Mexican signatures.

FOLLOWING PAGES (152–153)
José de Yturbe brings color, texture, and, above all, visual drama to his commercial architecture. Massive intersecting planes of bright color are punctuated by patterns of light and shadow cast by traditional overhead timber beams, geometric cutouts, floor patterns, and by the ever-present Mexican ingredient of flowing water.

FOLLOWING PAGES (154–155)
Mexican architecture as still life. The extraordinary scale of this yellow-bordered window cutout is revealed by the person walking behind the glass.

FOLLOWING PAGE (156)
Even in a hidden corner, Yturbe has arranged a simple collection of river stones against a bright yellow wall.

ACKNOWLEDGMENTS

Many people helped to make this book a reality. Manuel Mestre, talented architect, passionate enthusiast of Mexican culture, and friend, opened so many doors that it is difficult to imagine the book without his help, advice, and support. Similarly, Ana Cecilia Cortina went out of her way to make my impossible schedule possible. In Mexico City, the Camino Real Hotel became my second home, where I had the benefit of Carolina Mijares's experience and generous help from Mónica Díaz regarding official permissions. When it came to processing my film, all the people at LMI (Laboratorio Mexicano de Imagenes) could not have been more helpful, and they did great work. All the cooperation and assistance of the architects and their clients, museum managers, curators, and government officials I met along the way was very much appreciated. They included Tatiana Parcero, Catalina Corcuera, Norma Soto, Andrés Casillas, Dolores Olmedo, José de Yturbe, Lucio Muniain, Javier Sordo Madaleno, Enrique Martin Moreno, Abraham Maldonado, and Leonor Ortiz Monasterio. Finally, a special mention goes to Tim Street-Porter and his book *Casa Mexicana*, and to Isabel Goldsmith and her idyllic creation, Las Alamandas. Both provided me with enduring inspiration.

BIBLIOGRAPHY

Artes de Mexico, Mexico City. No. 7, "Neuva Epoca" (1993); No. 19, "Los Textiles de Chiapas" (1993); No. 23, "En el Mundo de Luis Barragán" (1994); No. 27, "El Tequila" (1994).

Coe, Michael D. *Mexico*. New York: Thames and Hudson, 1994.

Díaz del Castillo, Bernal. *The Conquest of New Spain*. Translated by J. M. Cohen. Harmondsworth: Penguin Books, 1993.

Portugal, Armando Salas. *Luis Barragán: The Architecture of Light, Color, and Form*. New York: Rizzoli, 1992.

Sayer, Chloë. *The Arts and Crafts of Mexico*. San Francisco: Chronicle Books, 1990. London: Thames and Hudson, 1990.

Sayer, Chloë. *Mexican Textiles*. London: Thames and Hudson, 1985.

Street-Porter, Tim. *Casa Mexicana: The Architecture, Design and Style of Mexico*. New York: Stewart, Tabori & Chang, 1989.

Townsend, Richard F. *The Aztecs*. New York: Thames and Hudson, 1993.

Yampolsky, Mariana. *The Traditional Architecture of Mexico*. New York: Thames and Hudson, 1993.

Zamora, Martha. *Frida Kahlo: The Brush of Anguish*. San Francisco: Chronicle Books, 1990.

MODERN

MAIOLICA

Forget Wedgwood. The dinnerware most prized in Mexico today is without doubt that produced by the artisan Gorki González in the old Colonial town of Guanajuato. Painstakingly made by hand, using methods and materials that have been employed for hundreds of years, his plates, cups, saucers, bowls, pots, and jugs are eagerly collected by discerning Mexicans, for they know that the craftsmanship of Señor González ensures that these one-off pieces will be the antiques of tomorrow. Foreign Traders of Santa Fe sell his work, alongside a range of quality antique and contemporary Mexican ceramics and furniture.

Tel. 1-505-983-6441
Fax 1-505-989-8917

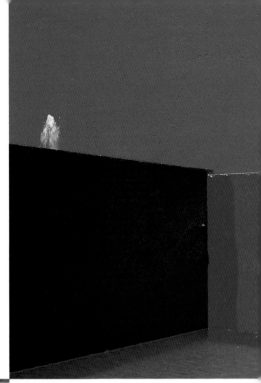

TALAVERA

TILES

*Mexicans took the technique of **talavera** or glazing from the Spanish and made it their own. The Indian love of fanciful decoration and bright color was brought to the manufacture of glazed tiles in the city of Puebla, tile-making center of Mexico. As a result, Mexican tiles have become renowned the world over for their vivid hues and captivating geometric and floral patterns. Still produced in Puebla by methods which were first introduced in early Colonial times, the "imperfect," hand-made character of **talavera** tiles continues to give them a broad appeal. Artesanos Imports of Santa Fe offer a generous range.*

Tel. 1-505-471-8020
Fax 1-505-471-8108

MEXICAN

PINK

Before Barragán, vast expanses of wall painted shocking pink would never have been considered "serious architecture." But Barragán had the conviction to use powerful colors that engaged the senses and emotions. His lesson was simple: a color that captures light can be used as a "tool," to highlight a space or to define an area. Why be afraid of color? Show no fear. Buy a pot of paint! And do as Barragán did: paint small patches of wall in different shades and decide later. Ralph Lauren's Santa Fe collection, available from Janovic Plaza, includes all the colors of Mexico.

Tel. 1-212-769-1440
1-800-379-7657

COLONIAL

SILVER

Silver and gold have been part of Mexico's craft tradition since ancient times. The Spaniards, presented with extravagant creations in gold and silver by Montezuma, were in awe of the skills of the Mexica (Aztecs). Silver mining made Colonial towns such as Guanajuato very affluent, and the craft of silverworking continues to flourish, albeit in styles very different from those of pre-Hispanic times. Here, plain silver plates, white ceramic bowls, and green apples are combined to create a typically Mexican still life. The best simple plates and platters in silver currently available are in the Calvin Klein homeware collection.

Tel. 1-212-292-9000
1-800-294-7978

AGUA

ARTE

A house without a fountain was unimaginable to Luis Barragán. His attitude was more eastern than western: fountains were "a source of peace, joy and restful sensuality"; spaces were "purified" by the musical flow of water. A fountain needed be no more than an occasional drop of water trickling into a stone bowl from an open pipe. This modernist fountain is just two intersecting walls, painted **azul añil** (deep blue), that frame and contain a small plume of water. The colors of Ralph Lauren's Santa Fe paint collection are the perfect backdrop to such a simple fountain (see "Mexican Pink"). Authentic Mexican fountains are available from Artesanos Imports of Santa Fe.

Tel. 1-505-471-8020
Fax 1-505-471-8108

GOLD

LEAF

Gold was used by the Aztecs more for its decorative appeal than as currency, and the importance of gold as the focal point of an interior continued with the extravagant altars of Catholic churches. So there is a healthy historical precedent for the gold-leaf paintings of Mathias Goeritz. The subtle patterns and captivating patina of gold leaf survive in Mexico today in the work of contemporary gold-leaf artisans. Perfectly suited to all-white modern interiors, gold paintings can be made by applying gold leaf to a painter's canvas. This example was created by the Mexican craftsman José Lira, based in Mexico City.

Tel. 011-52-5-762-1294

EQUIPAL

CHAIR

If there is one piece of furniture that cuts across every geographical, social, and economic boundary it is the Mexican equipal chair. Simply made from thin strips of woven timber with seat, back, and armrests covered in rugged leather, its appeal is similar to that of Mexican pottery and tiles—it is an item of craft that despite its popularity is still made entirely by hand. Found in just about every interior photographed for this book, the equipal chair is one of those rare items that bridge the gap between popular acceptance and good taste. Available from Artesanos Imports of Santa Fe.

Tel. 1-505-471-8020
Fax 1-505-471-8108

COTTON

COLOR

The ethno-historical data compiled by Friar Bernardino de Sahagún include a Toltec legend which tells of fields of cotton growing in colors of red, yellow, violet, green, white, and brown. Architect José de Yturbe invokes this mythology in the dining room of his new house, where blood-orange Mexican cotton covers the walls and table. A geometric arrangement of fruit and flowers completes a startlingly powerful still life that uses the simplest of ingredients. Designers' Guild produces a comprehensive range of brightly colored cottons, available through Osborne & Little.

Tel. 1-212-751-3333
Fax 1-212-752-6027

BENCH

STYLE

The tropical landscape of Mexico's Pacific coast has always demanded a different approach to architecture and design. The massive stone structures built by the Toltecs, Aztecs, or indeed the Catholic conquistadors would be completely out of place here. Simplicity reigns supreme. Decoration is kept to a minimum and most furniture is part of the architecture. At Las Alamandas, Isabel Goldsmith's idyllic coastal retreat, benches of color-rendered concrete and cushions covered with brightly colored Mexican cottons constitute the only real furniture. Designers' Guild fabrics, available through Osborne & Little, are all you need to complete your own Pacific simplicity.

Tel. 1-212-751-3333
Fax 1-212-752-6027

"Beauty is the oracle that speaks to us all."

Luis Barragán